What Is a California Se

Written by
Jack A. Graves

Illustrated by
Ralph W. Cooke III

Distributed by:

The Boxwood Press
P.O. Box 444
Pacific Grove, CA 93950
408—375-9110

ISBN: 0-910286-61-2

Second printing, 1978

Printed in U.S.A.

Dedicated to

Spencer, in whose hands, and those of his generation,
rests the awesome responsibility of preserving,
not only the sea otter, but all creatures,
whether threatened or not.

Preface

This book is written in a factual manner. The author's purpose is to inform the very young child about the California sea otter. It can be used as a "read to" book for pre-school children; most first, second, and third graders will be able to read it on their own. It is, indeed, geared for early childhood education (ECE)—age three to grade three. Because it has a science/social studies orientation, with an emphasis on ecology and environmental responsibilities, the book could very properly be used as the instigator for a unit on sea otters specifically, mammals generally, and/or the need for allowing the earth's creatures a proper and natural living environment.

The author has chosen this approach because he feels that today's children can understand more complex terminology and interpret generalizations about the importance of ecology, particularly when guided by a wise parent or teacher. Too, it is with these youngsters that the future of sea otters, and many other threatened or endangered species, will be decided. Rather than present this important theme in a traditional storybook form, the author has elected to write as he would talk with children in early childhood education—factually, honestly, and with warmth, friend-ship, and sincerity. The illustrations, so ably drawn by the artist, Ralph W. Cooke III of Carmel, California, add to the authenticity of the text by their charming and realistic qualities.

The author is familiar with elementary education and curriculum, having taught in grades three through six for six years, having served as a school principal in kindergarten through grade six for five years, and having been a college professor in an elementary credential program for seven years. In the latter position he has had the prime responsibility for training teacher candidates to teach reading at the elementary school level. His degrees (Bachelor of Arts, Master of Arts, Doctor of Education) provide him with the academic background for selecting vocabulary, style, and information for the boys and girls in early childhood education.

His thanks are extended to Ralph W. (Bill) Cooke III, the artist, whose illustrations make the text come alive, and to Dr. and Mrs. Ralph Buchsbaum of the Boxwood Press, both of whom offered encouragement, advice, confidence, and friendship during the publication of this book.

Jack A. Graves

Turlock, California
Spring 1977

The artist thanks Drs. James A. Mattison, Jr., Karl W. Kenyon, Paul Wild, and Ralph Buchsbaum for their exceptional photographs of the sea otter, which provided inspiration for some of the illustrations in this book.

Ralph W. Cooke III

Carmel, California
Spring 1977

A California sea otter is a mammal that lives in the
Pacific Ocean, along the central California coast.
It is found close to the shore.

It is friendly . . . and playful . . . and a joy to watch.

There are males and females, both young and old.

Some sea otters weigh as much as 30 kilograms,
about the same as this German shepherd dog.

4   Often sea otters live alone.

Or they live in groups, called *rafts*, of 30 or more animals.

Kelp is home
for the otters.

Kelp is a giant brown seaweed that grows upward from the ocean floor to the surface of the water. The stems, called *stipes,* are sometimes 30 meters tall.

It protects the young ... makes a fine bed ... and is a great place to find food.

While kelp benefits the sea otter, the otter, in turn, helps the kelp by eating sea urchins, which eat large amounts of kelp.

The kelp is shelter and food for sea snails, crabs, and abalones, as well as sea urchins.

8   Sea otters eat about one fourth of their weight daily. A 20-kilogram otter needs about 5 kilograms of food every day.

The sea otter eats, and eats, and eats!
It eats crabs, sea stars, sea urchins, snails, clams, mussels, and abalones.

It is fun to watch a sea otter eat.

It is on its back most of the time, and so this is how it has its dinner. Lying on its back, the sea otter uses its chest as a table.

Sometimes it will crack open a hard clam shell by pounding it against a rock placed on its chest.

The sea otter is very clever to use a stone as a tool.

Sometimes a seagull will follow an otter while it is eating ...

... and will snatch food right off the furry "table"!

After eating, the sea otter turns over and over in the water to wash away bits of food that cling to the hairs of its chest. Then the sea otter grooms itself.

Grooming is very important to keep its thick fur clean. The otter blows air into the spaces between the hairs. This keeps the cold water—which sometimes is as low as 9 degrees Celsius—away from the skin. If the cold water got to the sea otter's skin, its body temperature—normally 38 degrees Celsius—could fall. The sea otter has no thick layer of fat to help keep it warm, as do all other sea mammals, such as seals and whales.

16 After grooming, the sea otter wraps kelp around
its body. Securely anchored by the kelp,
the otter goes to sleep,
rocked by the waves
but safe from
drifting out
to sea.

Baby sea otters, called *pups*, are born in the winter of the year. The mother takes care of the pup, cleaning and nursing it.

Pups are born in the sea. This is because most sea otters stay in the water all their lives.

Rarely do California sea otters come onto the land.

The pup cannot swim at all and must ride on the chest of its mother. When she dives for food, she puts the pup on the surface of the water.

The pup bounces like a cork while waiting for its mother to come back. Sometimes it gets frightened and makes cries for her which sound much like those of a human infant.

The pup takes milk from its mother as does any other mammal. It gradually learns to eat solid food, which the mother shares with her baby.

After about two months the pup can swim on its own and soon will be able to dive for food.

Life was not always easy for the happy sea otter.

Many years ago it was hunted for its fur. The fur was
used for such things as fancy hats because
it was so soft and warm, and it lasted
a long time. Almost a million
of these trusting animals were
killed for their
soft fur!

Now, because people care, the sea otter lives a protected life. There are almost two thousand sea otters living in waters off the coast of central California. That may not sound like a lot—but just 40 years ago, there were only about 100 California sea otters.

It is great fun to sit by the ocean with binoculars and watch the sea otters eating, grooming, sleeping, and playing.

One good place to do this is along the shores of Monterey Bay, California.

Scientists are learning more about the life of the sea otter. Sometimes they capture them by using a harmless trap. Then they tag the sea otter to find out where it travels, what it eats, and how long it lives.

There are some dangers the sea otter must face, such as oil, chemicals used to clean boats, and engine propellers.

We should all help protect these animals.

If we do this, it is more likely that the sea otters will remain safe now, and be there for all of us—and future generations—to enjoy.

If there were no sea otters, we would not be able to watch them dive, use tools, and eat off their chests. What a sad thing *that* would be.

And now you know what
a California sea otter is!

About the author . . .

Dr. Jack A. Graves has been involved in elementary education for almost twenty years—six as a teacher, five as a principal, and seven as a college professor. He holds a Bachelor of Arts, with distinction, from Arizona State University, and Master of Arts and Doctor of Education degrees from the University of California, Berkeley. At present he is Professor of Education at California State College, Stanislaus, in Turlock, California, where he teaches elementary reading methods classes and graduate seminars in reading diagnosis and remediation. He serves as Director of the Division of Education's Reading Improvement Center, designed to assist elementary school youngsters in improving their reading capabilities. Besides observing sea otters from the shores of central California for over ten years and reading many publications on the mammal, he has taken a professional study course about the otter from the University of California, Santa Cruz. Among his many memberships are the International Reading Association, the California Reading Association, the Stanislaus Reading Council, and Friends of the Sea Otter.

About the artist . . .

Ralph William (Bill) Cooke III is a lifetime resident of Carmel, California, where he has received his art education from an early age. A student in several schools in the Monterey Peninsula area, he was influenced by many fine artist-teachers. He studied independently in Europe, and developed his skills in pen and ink for the last five of his twenty-three years. He has received awards in California and Arizona. His original drawings have been displayed by Carmel Galleries, and some are in many private collections. He is now an illustrator in the Naval Postgraduate School in Monterey. Bill has spent many hours in rowboats on Monterey Bay observing and photographing the sea otter. His love for the otters and their environment adds a special flavor to the drawings for this book.